T0209749

IN THE PEWS

Delfred Rodgers

authorHOUSE®

AuthorHouse™
1663 Liberty Drive
Bloomington, IN 47403
www.authorhouse.com
Phone: 1 (800) 839-8640

Published by AuthorHouse 08/24/2019

ISBN: 978-1-7283-2424-1 (sc)
ISBN: 978-1-7283-2423-4 (e)

Library of Congress Control Number: 2019912401

Print information available on the last page.

American Standard Version (ASV)
Public Domain

King James Version (KJV)
Public Domain

New Living Translation (NLT)
Holy Bible, New Living Translation, copyright © 1996, 2004, 2015 by Tyndale House Foundation. Used by permission of Tyndale House Publishers, Inc., Carol Stream, Illinois 60188. All rights reserved.

FOREWORD

As a child we played near this large house that was only occupied on the weekends. There was a basketball court and the grass fluffy, and green. There was a sign on the gate that stated, "No Trespassing", but as a child in the neighborhood we did not consider the locked gate as a do not enter. Instead as children we climbed the fence and played after school. The large house was in our neighborhood, there were no dogs guarding the home, so we just played and saw the location as a safe play-ground for children.

One summer my grandmother was in town visiting for vacation. My grandmother, a minister that loved Jesus Christ informed me that I was seen by her playing on the secured church grounds. We discussed the reasoning of the church and why I was not allowed to be on a closed site. I listened to her reasoning and obeyed her instructions to not be on a secured site. My friends began to tease me and call me names because I no longer was behind the secured gates of the large home, defined as "The Church House."

As a child I was raised in a segregated community until we moved in the late 1960's. I did not attend local church regularly, and there was no understanding of what church represented. The elementary school I attended was a racially mixed Christian school where God was the center piece, but as a child I did not understand why I did not go to the same school as my friends on the same block. There was respect learned as a youth for people and property, but the large house location "The Church House" was considered as an oasis for basketball games for the youth in my neighborhood. The activities at this church were always fun and involved the children. I only attended church meetings on Sunday, when I was asked by my friends. Some Sundays, my mother would attend a church on the northside of town where I had no relationships, and just pondered in the seats, called Pews.

As I continued to mature and entered college, I found myself further distancing myself from "The Church House." The location of places, buildings similar to "The Church House" where I grew up was a complete mystery. I had a desire to attend the church meetings in college, but when attended I just sat in the seat of the church called Pews. The gathering of church I experienced had no social contact beyond the walls. I would get to church meetings early to enjoy the choir singing. The messages were inspiring, but the scriptures in the Bible lacked meaning that changed my getting closer to "The Church House."

I continued to party and enjoy the fun shared outside of the church. I attend church every now and then, but there was no deep desire to be active and leave the Pew. One day, I attended church service and a visiting speaker talked on a topic that got my full attention. When the speaker asked for altar call, I got up from that Pew and conversed to the speaker, intently. I gave my life to Jesus that day, but the lack of socialization continued, and having a mentor to assist me to understand Bible scripture was stressful. I consciously left the Pew to learn and become active, but I had trouble understanding the message. I got extremely radical in my quiet time and asked the Holy Spirit to help me to know who he is.

I pray that this short book will help you fellowship with other folk you do not know, especially those that find refuge at your church. There are people in your congregation that seek friendships, just like you. We would like to think we were not torn on the inside, but we are all dysfunctional in our directions until we meet and accept the Holy Spirit. I am planting a seed or watering your thoughts, so get out of the Pews.

CHAPTER 1

Beginnings

I remember going to church as a child and hearing noise—loud shouting, singing, people dancing, and a "praise the Lord" as a normal greeting. The Pews were wooden benches and in orderly rows. Back then, up until the mid-1980s, there was a picture of white Jesus Christ on the wall that still exists in many churches today. I often wondered who this person was, because there were similar pictures in this book everyone used called the **BIBLE**. It appeared that everyone focused on the picture, as Jesus (God in the flesh). As a child, I often wondered how and why this picture of the Son of God could be God, and no one can see God and live (**Exodus 33:20**). I was not allowed to argue about unbelief as a child, but as I got older (a teenager) and became woven in the church environment, I began to see life differently, so that I questioned the picture, the church thought, and why the front cover of my Bible had that picture as the Son of God.

There were so many needs deeply stamped in my environment and the Biblical stories preached on Sunday, to me, lacked a clear answer, and did not relate with me. As a young adult in college, I needed something to balance my life desires, as I was hearing different doctrinal philosophies about life everywhere (**1 Timothy 4:16).** So many things negated, yet confirmed, some of the doctrine I'd grown up with. Yet, I was confused. I decided to go back to the church house and visit (I was 18 years old). This was a place where my parents took me on occasion: Christmas, Mother's Day, and Easter.

The Sunday I went to church, the speaker/preacher of the hour was talking about his life as a teen into adulthood, and I listened intently. When he said, "Come, taste and see of the Lord Jesus Christ," I went down to the altar, because finally, I had heard about a caring relationship with the Spirit (**Psalm 34:8)**. I heard that this Spirit was Holy, because it came from God and His Spirit would guide my life and be with me until the end of the world. (**1 John 2:27**).

I got baptized in water that day. But then the challenges of what I heard in the world became very clear, and the sin I had hoped would go away seemed easier to attain within the environments where I wandered. There was a real battle in my mind. I tried to make friends with other men in the church, but it seemed we could not connect. Nobody called me or invited me to church gatherings. I showed up at church events and felt isolated. These instances contributed to my decision to return to my old way of living (as a young adult in college, parties and worldly fun ran rampant). Being in a fraternity was a strong affirmation of campus involvement, so I adopted some of my fraternity brother's lifestyles. The lessons I heard were hard to understand from church and were not a part of my life. Folk from church wanted me to be something I did not understand, and no one took time to share with me the Biblical teaching, so I continued to do what I believed was cool. I definitely could have been involved deeper into a sinful life. It's not easy to be around sin and not desire the prize of that life, but I know now it was the Holy Spirit that kept me away from going too far into sin. (**Ephesians 4:22-32).** In this book, I will share some of my testimony, which reflects how many people contemplate the choice to serve God or serve the world (**Matthew 6:24**). Many people that go to church define the world culture as sin—a complete opposite of good and acceptable unto God, and truly believe that just being in the Pews for church is the answer. Well, from your reading of this short book, I pray God will reveal your purposed destiny in Him (the Creator of Heaven and Earth).

We occupy space...actively working, raising a family, enjoying our hobbies, or doing something in this world; the demand of time in the flesh wars against the Spirit man and opposes the purposes of God. (**Galatians 5:17**). Just think what it would be like doing the will of God (seeking the purpose He has chosen for you, guided by the Holy Spirit). Spend some quality time with the Holy Spirit and allow the power of God's Spirit to help you remember the purpose He gave you. I pray the father in Heaven, in Jesus Christ's name, will resurrect your God-given gift for the Kingdom of God, so it can be used unto God (**Ephesians 2:8-10).**

CHAPTER 2

Finding the treasure map

I often wonder how people think, as they walk into the church house. Really, I wonder the thought, when the gathering of people come together. Is it to see the presence of God? (**Acts 1:1-5**)

I remember when I came to church earlier in my life, seeking God. I believed that I would have my prayer met at that meeting. The problem I had was staying focused on my prayer. My mind was floating with thoughts of how to make money in this society, dating, completing school, and hanging out at a level to be accepted among friends. If I could have come to church blindfolded and sought God, then the many things I saw on my way to church would not have limited my energy to seek God (**Romans 10: 2-3**).

The treasure map over the years has led me to now use my praise, and that praise (forgetting all my issues and problems) leads me into the gates of worship (**Psalms 100).** To allow this mind to focus, you have to feed on the Holy desire deep within you, and that depth comes from prayer—a daily relationship with the Spirit of God, reading and meditating on the Word of God, The Bible (**Colossians 1:9).**

To decode the treasure map and make correct steps and turns for my life, I constantly train my brain to understand the desire must be about the Kingdom of God. I may not see the direction physically, but I stay focused and continue asking the Holy Spirit for direction and guiding safety (**Psalm 51).**

When we lack relationship with God, our direction from the Holy Spirit can be cloudy. When we do not believe God, then the Holy Spirit cannot live in our bodies, thus the environment we live in leads us away from God. Making decisions in life can be cloudy without the Holy Spirit. The Holy Spirit lives inside our bodies, when we accept God and when we allow the Holy Spirit to lead by making decisions for us, we always win. When a decision needs to be made, allow the Holy Spirit within you to make the right call. God wants us to seek the Kingdom of God first (**Matthew 6:33**). We must realize we are in the Earth realm—a place that is physical. Thus, we cannot rely on our human nature to prove a Holy God exists (**John 15:5).** God is the creator of all things, and we must first acknowledge our inability without God, and our ability with God, in Spirit. Seeking is searching everything the Bible says and moving based only on the guidance and direction the Holy Spirit leads you through. It is a very humbling experience to let the past experiences and knowledge learned from the world be stripped from your mind, but you must allow God to direct the very essence of your being today and tomorrow (**Proverbs 3:6).**

The Pews are a place (church or courtroom) where we sit down and allow the words from the pulpit to shower our thoughts. We are only discussing the church and the Kingdom of Heaven in the Pews. When a person is unlearned by not practicing what is stated in the Bible, they need assistance with scriptures and the Holy Spirit is available to intercede with prayer. I know when I came to church to fellowship as an adult, it appeared that most everyone understood the Word of God. However, as I began to practice what I had read, I noticed that some folk really lacked a basic understanding of who Jesus Christ is and his mission on earth. Jesus' body as man died for the redemption for all sins. When Jesus died, he became the bridge in the gap to God. Because of the Jesus' death, we can now believe and have faith in the name of Jesus Christ that gives man a choice to live eternally with God. It was years before I began to recondition my mind, and it began in the Pews of a church house, a battleground I never knew existed (**Ephesians 4:23).**

I was a watcher, a person that learned when to say, "Amen," when to stand, and when and how to shout. I wanted to be a part of what the pulpit was preaching. I wanted the Holy Ghost. I would move and huddle up with others after church in groups that allowed me to exist (be a groupie) and hear topics that had nothing to do with the message just preached from the pulpit (**II Timothy 3:5).** Women would be looking – sometimes blatantly staring at me. There were very few men that came and greeted me, even after being in the church house for a few months. There was no fellowship (**1 Corinthians 10:24**) for a new person. Bible class was often non-relational to me; the facilitating teacher never really opened my mind's desire to go deeper and understand. When I came to church, I sought sobriety to change from the world. The world had my attention: sports, women, alcohol, parties, and very few of the folks I communicated with knew what the church was designed for and had a reverence for what was in the building (usher, choir, preaching, etc.) (**Ephesians 5:19**), instead of seeking the Holy Spirit. This made my understanding of church even more complicated, because I only sought what was in the church building (usher, choir, preaching, etc.). I saw nothing in the church house to draw me closer to God. There was a yelling preacher, good music, pretty women, few men, a picture of a man they called Jesus (that suppressed my race), and a good chicken or barbecue dinner after church (that I took home, due to lack of fellowship). I really had a need to understand the truth and meaning in the physical church building (**Hebrews 10:24-26**). So, Sunday after Sunday, I repeated the same activities, not understanding what I read and having no friends or associates to discuss these concepts of church. So, I just sat in the Pews, believing I was okay with my life (**John 15:4**), but understanding nothing, I was disconnected. There was a treasure map, the Bible, and I had no clue of how to use it.

CHAPTER 3

Digging for the Treasure (Seed)

In college, there were many obstacles that took my mind off the race for Jesus Christ (Jesus is the one I eventually found to be my treasure seed). Not understanding the Bible nor having a friend with a true relationship in the Holy Spirit who could share with me what I was reading frustrated me. As a first-year college student, I decided to go to church. Few of my friends were attending church, and my best friend Ron, who took me to church with him occasionally as a child, was attending a college about 300 miles away. I really missed him because we would go to church together and sing in his aunt's choir. I often admired my dear friend because he appeared to have a balanced life. Ron used to share with me his vision of the Kingdom of God and why being truthful and forgiving to everyone is so important. Before meeting my friend, I had learned academic experiences from Christian parochial school, but he felt like one of the only people I could talk to about my relationship with God (**Proverbs 11:24-25**).

When I pledged my fraternity, they had recognized Christian beliefs, yet few around my campus walked in them. One of the fraternity founders held the office of Bishop in a church. Many of the brothers I went to college with knew of God but did not know Him in relationship (**John 15:7**). Like most people, we had learned behavior, and many of the habits of the world I attained came from my inner circle of brothers in college. To this day I find myself still pulling the weeds in my mind daily, just so I can focus on what God has purposed for me (**Galatians 5:13**). Consistent desire to know the Holy Spirit led me to a place of security in knowing God.

Today, daily relationships with God make me take a moment, because I am accustomed to reading the newspaper with a cup of coffee first thing in the morning. My alternative is now to pray, where I give thanks to God for getting me through yesterday and blessing me for this day to be a beacon of light for others as I go through the day, (**Philemon 5-6**). I had to learn that God promises this protection. Every step you take forward knowing the light is in you, darkness must take a step out of your way and allow the light to shine (**Hebrews 12:28-29**).

Some folk come to church with a mystical mind-set (witchcraft-not knowing), and when a person lacks knowing and having a Godly relationship, the map to understanding His ways become cloudy, (**Isaiah 55:8**). God says to just believe in Him. We find this belief as we seek the Kingdom of God and all his righteousness (**Matthew 6:33).** Many men I know run away from the Word of God (Bible) versus running toward the Word of God.

hint: This is a light and path to righteousness.

When I came to church, I thought God was in my praise, but then forgot the worship because I really was lacking relationship. You see our worship (relationship in knowing God) should ignite the praise to God (**Psalms 148:14).** The testimony of our belief of wanting to have a relationship with God will grow. That growth (seed) is the power of the Holy Ghost in you that wants to guide your steps through life (**II Corinthians 5:7).** Many folks are around the treasure but stop there. We come to church with myths, identifying physical things, but lacking the worship (relationship with God) to settle and remain where God has a blessing for us. Church assemblage is a good place to be, but the altar of your heart where God speaks through man needs to know this Spirit and Truth (This is known by a daily relationship with God). The questions that should be answered from the Pews should be, "How I can get in Spirit and find Truth?" Well the Spirit and Truth are "one", and a person should be mentally ready to hear truth at church assembly. I became mentally ready by reading the word and searching for clues led by the Holy Spirit (**Romans 12:1.** When my mind allowed the physical body to be a vessel (representing the Kingdom of God with their mind-body), then there was a growing effect of that truth seed that took root in righteousness (representing the kingdom of God). As the root got stronger with the living Word, the power of that growth realized right from wrong and spoke with faith (action) to questions that did not represent the Kingdom of God (**Colossians 3:1-4).**

This learning experience is the greatest position of gaining God's light to grow (**II Peter 3:18).** Similar to my uncharted path, it may be rocky (difficult) reaching the treasure of knowing the Kingdom of God, but like I did, you will grow in God, trusting your learning, and continuing to find support digging in the Word of God; that becomes your treasure (**Psalms 91**). I started asking the Holy Spirit, "Is this the Fellowship Church for my life? (**Hebrews 10:25).** Is this where you want me to be, Holy Spirit? Holy Spirit, are these the people you want me to associate with and continue to dig for treasure searching the Kingdom of God? Is the leader openly sharing with me the gifts of the Kingdom of God that the Holy Spirit has given freely to share, and thus using their talent to stunt my gift for their benefit and misdirect my growth?" I know there are multiple other questions, but the key is digging for the treasures in the Kingdom of God and continuing to find Heavenly nuggets that prove in the Word of God that the path is a straight path (**Proverbs 4:26).** I had to learn every day, getting closer to that purpose of God in my life (**Matthew 6:33).**

CHAPTER 4

Plant the Seed – Garden for growth

What tool do you use when you work in the yard or garden? I mostly use a soft touch hand trowel (a miniature shovel). The tool allows me to dig out unwanted growth around my plants and gives me the ability to dig up unwanted weeds from the root. When I am studying the word of God I have my tools (a reference Bible, and message Bible or different NIV versions), so I can clearly get to the core of the Scripture (seed or 'the nugget') planted deep in me (the garden of my heart) so I can meditate on the word daily (**Genesis 2:15-16).**

I cannot come to church with a "no matter what I hear," thought, and "I am still going to do what I want to do mentality." No! Please, come to church no matter the issues needing answers, and come with the willingness to allow the

Holy Spirit to change the thinking, and permeate the very core of ideas forming in the mind for Kingdom building (**Romans 12:1-2**). I was really confused with thoughts of spirituality coming from many directions. I had trouble with dividing truth, all things in my garden had to be uprooted to allow me to be guided by the Holy Spirit and find the consciousness of truth. I challenged and tested God and didn't have to; I was so immature. As a Christian, allowing the Holy Spirit to lead me, I could easily see the weeds growing and the need to pull the weeds out of my life (**Matthew 13:24-43**).

1. **a house garden:** a piece of ground, and often near a house, used for growing-flowers, fruit, or vegetables (yard, plot or bed of dirt, patch, lawn).

To have a garden representing the Kingdom of God, the Faith seeds from God must be planted deep in good soil in the garden (in your heart), and any insects, weeds, birds, or other outside influences that can affect the growth of the seeds of the God must be removed from the garden, from the root (**Ephesians 3:10, 17**).

2. **cultivation:** an action word for working in a garden. The process of trying to acquire or develop a quality or skill.

Based on the process of cultivating daily you will grow the seeds (Bible truth) in your garden. Again, the de-weeding (removing a plant that is considered undesirable, unattractive, or troublesome that grows where it is not wanted) must take place daily. This process is a major issue that damages the young growth of a seed (**Mark 4:32).**

When I go to church, it is largely because I am; 1) a growing seed, 2) a seed that likes being around other similar seeds, 3) a seed that needed to be planted in soil, but is sometimes not planted deep enough in the garden, or 4) a seed that grows, but the growing process has been tampered in growth. Therefore, a person or church must love all seeds, and be open to assist the adopted seed that needs to grow in the garden by sharing the Word of God and praying (**Psalms 37:25, I Corinthians 6:19).**

CHAPTER 5

Our God is so transparent; on the six day he stated: "let us make man in our own image": (this is an intransitive representative to create).

When I try and duplicate our Father's statement, I look in the mirror at my flesh and speak, "God is a Spirit in me", and God made this statement - **(Genesis 1:26).** Only he can create and speak life into my body. We must have a mind of Christ, **(John 15:15).** We must be as bold as our Eternal Father in Heaven, because we cannot see in the Spirit-realm. We must believe the Bible and Trust the Word our light that strengthens our Faith, **(John 12:35-36).** God spoke the Word, and in that Word was made flesh, and only God knows all about us. When Jesus Christ became the son of man and took all sins and temptations that kept us from reining in the Earth realm to the cross, we just have to believe and continue to seek understanding in the birth-death-resurrection of Jesus Christ. (**Philippians 3:15-16).**

The Bible is clear stating: "that as, much as we see the end approaching, we should assemble ourselves." Assemblage is pulling all the parts of the body that believes God's Word and know that "God is" as one unit, under the will of God against the forces of evil, (**Ephesians 6:12-13**). This obedience to do what the Holy Spirit (that lives in the believer) tells me to do, is life. Thus, when I am not walking in the Holy Spirit according to the Bible, I am in sin and have no power, (**Romans 5:12).**

Many folk are in the Pews lacking understanding of the Bible; either a) the person is not reading the Word of God for confirmation of what the preacher stated, or / and b) the person is running the race of life without accountability (a prayer partner who they can share issues with), so sin is highly active because no one can identify the person›s character, or / and C) the person comes to church to watch people and spreads the deadness of their thoughts to other folk who are also negative, and also struggling, (**James 1:22).**

To hide the sin in your life is a crime, there is a fugitive in your body (spirit not like God controlling your mind and body) that can take residence and abide in your body. You cannot serve two Masters "either you hate one master and love the other," (**Matthew 6:24**). Without reading God's Word daily, praying and asking the Holy Spirit to guide your life, and stay in FAITH, the illuminated road for your life begins to disappear to God's eternal direction becoming shaded. The mind will begin to accept the world culture as a guide, (**James 5:3).**

Anything not like God is an enemy and a spiritual fugitive lurking in the Temple (physical body), where the Holy Spirit lives, (**I Corinthians 6:19-20**). Look we all have a sin nature, but you must die out (completely-walking and training daily in FAITH of our Lord and Savior Jesus Christ) and not allow sin to have any place in our lives.

I found that consciousness must be learned on the fruits of the Holy Spirit and look forward to the gifts of the Holy Spirit reigning and teaching us how to live in that gift daily, (**Galatians 5:16, 22-23**). The Bible states the church is the bride of Christ, (**Revelations 19:7).** The church must worship God (give thanks) for what he has done, and the purpose to do Kingdom of God work through your life. When we all come together at church on one-accord and enjoy the Holy Spirit as the main attraction there is a sharing from God - his manna (food – Word) from Heaven. We can experience (healing, change in the way we see a situation, power to overcome a situation), (**Acts 2:38).**

I remember sitting in the Pews and when I first believed God. The Holy Spirit entered my entire body with a will to know God. My mind began to listen more intently, it took me decades, but I just excepted the Holy Spirt and my heart thoughts actually began to change. I began to go to church and sit in that same area of where that Pew was that day. The more I listened to the preached Word and confirmed the Scripture by reading the Word of God, and praying for guidance, and understanding in the Word of God with meditating on the Word of God the stronger I became a soldier in God's Army, (**Romans 10:17**).

Through the power of the Holy Spirit, I was able to remember and quote meaningful Bible Scriptures, only God could allow my mind to recall, (**Psalm 34:8**). When I tasted the goodness of who God, is when I learned wisdom by fearing God and understanding the fear of God is staying away from evil, (**Proverbs 9:10).**

Any good fruit that is sweet comes from a well-maintained tree, where the care-taker labored to keep the weeds and bugs from destroying the fruit until it reaches maturity of harvest, (**II Thessalonians 3:3).** Allow the seed of faith the Word of God in you, the unmerited favors-(gifts from God is his grace), to keep you attached to that heavenly place in Jesus Christ (**Ephesians 1:3).** Jesus came as God in the flesh (son of man – the 2nd Adam) and was born with God's DNA - (**John 1:1, 14**), and with his death on the cross, at Cavalry - Skull (Golgotha Hill), and His resurrection on the third day from a borrowed tomb with all Victory. Jesus Christ is the only acceptable sacrifice for man and sits on the mercy seat as the atonement for man's sin as the advocated representation in the Eternal-realm, **(Ephesians 2:18).** Asking in Jesus name and recognizing the blessing that God is the only way, we can call God our father, (**I Corinthians 12:3).** I earnestly confess, you must be born again (surrender your old way of living life – stop trusting the answer to come by the flesh), and the Holy Spirit will enter in and life will begin to be seen from a different level and perspective. From the Pews there should be evidence of spiritual activity somewhere in the body of believers, where you assemble. Command the physical mind and body to give the Holy Spirit permission to be the guide. The Holy Spirit will take residence in you and lead, making you a witness to others while growing in Jesus Christ by FAITH. Eventually Wisdom grows so understanding of our father is clearer, and the testimony of the Holy Spirit will evangelize to others in and outside the church assembly. You are the church of the living God, it lives in you. You are in the PEWS!

CHAPTER 6

Conclude:

While in the Pews our eyes see all kinds of things that send thoughts to our mind, some are not of God and they have a way to hinder our connection to God, while we are sitting in the Pews, right in the church house. Melodies of some songs in the church house touch our mind and make us want to react to the call of the Word of God, but in an instant something around you says don't give praise and worship to God. Perhaps if you lift up your hands, stand, applause to the little belief you hear from the Holy Spirit that small flicker of flame within you, can engulf, then the Holy Spirit can answer your questions through the Word of God.

Again, my connection to getting out of the Pews was due to my desire to know beyond my thought, who God is? Unlike me, you may not have had a roller-coaster decisioned life, but regardless, of my choices the Holy Spirit always had an answer to my problems. Sometimes the answer was immediate, and there are some answers the Holy Spirit delayed. There are many answers that await my growth in knowing the Kingdom of God, but I continue to search solace in the Word of God. You cannot come to the church-house and be stagnant, get in a men's choir, men's Bible study, men's fellowship - the same for women until you feel strong enough in the Spirit of God to walk an issue out. It may take sharing your issues with a prayer partner you have entrusted, as they share the Word of God. Get out of the Pews, (Stop!) just being a spiritual Zombie that comes out to be seen as a Christian, lacking a relationship with the eternal God.

The Pew in the church-house was meant to be a place to rest your flesh and allow the Spirit to hear from God in a physical realm. The heavenly realm is a constant battle-ground for your soul. Unless, you are walking in FAITH your soul is open to eternal damnation. Get out of the Pews having a secret life and open your heart to the Holy Spirit.

It is okay, you can get out of the Pews and learn of the great Love God has for you, through Jesus Christ. Be mentored by the person who brought you to church, through them you will meet others and find a ministry where you feel led by the Holy Spirit to be active. Remember the Church is a garden of many different seeds. Some seek God's Spiritual purpose, and others are not seeking God. God is the Creator of all things & establishes your root, stay attached to the root and allow God to produce you to maturity. Amen

NOTES

Bible Scripture – Support

Beginnings

1 - [20] And he said, Thou canst not see my face; for man shall not see me and live.

Ex 33:20 (ASV)

2 - [16] Take heed to thyself, and to thy teaching. Continue in these things; for in doing this thou shalt save both thyself and them that hear thee.

1 Tim 4:16 (ASV)

[8] O taste and see that the Lord *is* good: blessed *is* the man *that* trusteth in him.

Psalms 34:8 (KJV)

4 -[27] But you have received the Holy Spirit, and he lives within you, so you don't need anyone to teach you what is true. For the Spirit teaches you everything you need to

know, and what he teaches is true—it is not a lie. So just as he has taught you, remain in fellowship with Christ.

1 John 2:27 (NLT)

5 - [22] throw off your old sinful nature and your former way of life, which is corrupted by lust and deception.[23] Instead, let the Spirit renew your thoughts and attitudes.[24] Put on your new nature, created to be like God—truly righteous and holy.[25] So stop telling lies. Let us tell our neighbors the truth, for we are all parts of the same body.[26] And "don't sin by letting anger control you." Don't let the sun go down while you are still angry,[27] for anger gives a foothold to the devil.[28] If you are a thief, quit stealing. Instead, use your hands for good hard work, and then give generously to others in need.[29] Don't use foul or abusive language. Let everything you say be good and helpful, so that your words will be an encouragement to those who hear them.[30] And do not bring sorrow to God's Holy Spirit by the way you live. Remember, he has identified you as his own, guaranteeing that you will be saved on the day of redemption.[31] Get rid of all bitterness, rage, anger, harsh words, and slander, as well as all types of evil behavior.[32] Instead, be kind to each other, tenderhearted, forgiving one another, just as God through Christ has forgiven you.

Eph 4:22-32 (NLT)

6 - [24] "No one can serve two masters. For you will hate one and love the other; you will be devoted to one and despise the other. You cannot serve both God and money.

Matt 6:24 (NLT)

7 - [17] The sinful nature wants to do evil, which is just the opposite of what the Spirit wants. And the Spirit gives us desires that are the opposite of what the sinful nature desires. These two forces are constantly fighting each other, so you are not free to carry out your good intentions.

Gal 5:17 (NLT)

Finding the treasure map

8 - [8] God saved you by his grace when you believed. And you can't take credit for this; it is a gift from God. [9] Salvation is not a reward for the good things we have done, so none of us can boast about it. [10] For we are God's masterpiece. He has created us anew in Christ Jesus, so we can do the good things he planned for us long ago.

Eph 2:8-10 (NLT)

9 - [1] In my first book I told you, Theophilus, about everything Jesus began to do and teach [2] until the day he was taken up to heaven after giving his chosen apostles further instructions through the Holy Spirit. [3] During the forty days after his crucifixion, he appeared to the apostles from time to time, and he proved to them in many ways that he was actually alive. And he talked to them about the Kingdom of God. [4] Once when he was eating with them, he commanded them, "Do not leave Jerusalem until the Father sends you the gift he promised, as I told you before. [5] John baptized with water, but in just a few days you will be baptized with the Holy Spirit."

Acts 1:1-5 (NLT)

10 - ² I know what enthusiasm they have for God, but it is misdirected zeal.³ For they don't understand God's way of making people right with himself. Refusing to accept God's way, they cling to their own way of getting right with God by trying to keep the law

Romans 10:2-3 (NLT)

11 - ¹ Make a joyful noise unto the LORD, all ye lands. ² Serve the LORD with gladness: come before his presence with singing. ³ Know ye that the LORD he *is* God: *it is* he *that* hath made us, and not we ourselves; *we are* his people, and the sheep of his pasture. ⁴ Enter into his gates with thanksgiving, *and* into his courts with praise: be thankful unto him and bless his name. ⁵ For the LORD *is* good; his mercy *is* everlasting; and his truth *endureth* to all generations.

Psalms 100:1-5 (KJV)

12 - ⁹ So we have not stopped praying for you since we first heard about you. We ask God to give you complete knowledge of his will and to give you spiritual wisdom and understanding.

Col 1:9 (NLT)

13 - ¹ Have mercy upon me, O God, according to thy lovingkindness: according unto the multitude of thy tender mercies blot out my transgressions. ² Wash me thoroughly from mine iniquity and cleanse me from my sin. ³ For I acknowledge my transgressions: and my sin *is* ever before me. ⁴ Against thee, thee only, have I sinned, and done *this* evil in

thy sight: that thou mightiest be justified when thou speakest, *and* be clear when thou judgest. ⁵ Behold, I was shapen in iniquity; and in sin did my mother conceive me. ⁶ Behold, thou desirest truth in the inward parts: and in the hidden *part* thou shalt make me to know wisdom. ⁷ Purge me with hyssop, and I shall be clean: wash me, and I shall be whiter than snow. ⁸ Make me to hear joy and gladness; *that* the bones *which* thou hast broken may rejoice. ⁹ Hide thy face from my sins and blot out all mine iniquities. ¹⁰ Create in me a clean heart, O God; and renew a right spirit within me. ¹¹ Cast me not away from thy presence; and take not thy holy spirit from me. ¹² Restore unto me the joy of thy salvation; and uphold me *with thy* free spirit. ¹³ *Then* will I teach transgressors thy ways; and sinners shall be converted unto thee. ¹⁴ Deliver me from blood guiltiness, O God, thou God of my salvation: *and* my tongue shall sing aloud of thy righteousness. ¹⁵ O Lord open thou my lips; and my mouth shall shew forth thy praise. ¹⁶ For thou desirest not sacrifice; else would I give *it*: thou delightest not in burnt offering. ¹⁷ The sacrifices of God *are* a broken spirit: a broken and a contrite heart, O God, thou wilt not despise. ¹⁸ Do good in thy good pleasure unto Zion: build thou the walls of Jerusalem. ¹⁹ Then shalt thou be pleased with the sacrifices of righteousness, with burnt offering and whole burnt offering: then shall they offer bullocks upon thine altar.

Psalms 51:1-19 (KJV)

14 - ³³ Seek the Kingdom of God above all else, and live righteously, and he will give you everything you need.

Matt 6:33 (NLT)

15 - **5** "Yes, I am the vine; you are the branches. Those who remain in me, and I in them, will produce much fruit. For apart from me you can do nothing.

John 15:5 (NLT)

16 - **6** In all thy ways acknowledge him, and he shall direct thy paths.

Prov 3:6 (KJV)

17 - **23** Instead, let the Spirit renew your thoughts and attitudes.

Eph 4:23 (NLT)

18 - **5** They will act religious, but they will reject the power that could make them godly. Stay away from people like that!

2 Tim 3:5 (NLT)

19 - **24** But to those called by God to salvation, both Jews and Gentiles, Christ is the power of God and the wisdom of God.

1 Cor 1:24 (NLT)

20 - **19** speaking one to another in psalms and hymns and spiritual songs, singing and making melody with your heart to the Lord;

Eph 5:19 (ASV)

21 - 24 Let us think of ways to motivate one another to acts of love and good works. 25 And let us not neglect our meeting together, as some people do, but encourage one another, especially now that the day of his return is drawing near. 26 Dear friends, if we deliberately continue sinning after we have received knowledge of the truth, there is no longer any sacrifice that will cover these sins.

Heb 10:24-26 (NLT)

22 - 4 Remain in me, and I will remain in you. For a branch cannot produce fruit if it is severed from the vine, and you cannot be fruitful unless you remain in me.

John 15:4 (NLT)

III. Digging for the Treasure (Seed)

23 - 24 Give freely and become more wealthy; be stingy and lose everything.
25 The generous will prosper; those who refresh others will themselves be refreshed.

Prov 11:24-25 (NLT)

24 - 7 If ye abide in me, and my words abide in you, ask whatsoever ye will, and it shall be done unto you.

John 15:7 (ASV)

25 - 13 For you have been called to live in freedom, my brothers, and sisters. But don't use your freedom to satisfy

your sinful nature. Instead, use your freedom to serve one another in love.

Gal 5:13 (NLT)

26 - ⁵ because I keep hearing about your faith in the Lord Jesus and your love for all of God's people. ⁶ And I am praying that you will put into action the generosity that comes from your faith as you understand and experience all the good things we have in Christ.

Philemon 1:5-6 (NLT)

27 - ²⁸ Wherefore, receiving a kingdom that cannot be shaken, let us have grace, whereby we may offer service well-pleasing to God with reverence and awe: ²⁹ for our God is a consuming fire.

Heb 12:28-29 (ASV)

28 - ⁸ "My thoughts are nothing like your thoughts," says the LORD. "And my ways are far beyond anything you could imagine.

Isaiah 55:8 (NLT)

29 - ³³ Seek the Kingdom of God above all else, and live righteously, and he will give you everything you need.

Matt 6:33 (NLT)

30 - ¹⁴ And he hath lifted up the horn of his people, The praise of all his saints; Even of the children of Israel, a people near unto him. Praise ye Jehovah.

Psalms 148:14 (ASV)

31 - ⁷ (For we walk by faith, not by sight:)

2 Cor 5:7 (KJV)

32 - ¹ I beseech you therefore, brethren, by the mercies of God, to present your bodies a living sacrifice, holy, acceptable to God, *which is* your spiritual service.

Romans 12:1 (ASV)

33 - ¹ If then ye were raised together with Christ, seek the things that are above, where Christ is, seated on the right hand of God. ² Set your mind on the things that are above, not on the things that are upon the earth. ³ For ye died, and your life is hid with Christ in God. ⁴ When Christ, *who is* our life, shall be manifested, then shall ye also with him be manifested in glory.

Col 3:1-4 (ASV)

34 - ¹⁸ But grow in grace, and *in* the knowledge of our Lord and Saviour Jesus Christ. To him *be* glory both now and forever. Amen.

2 Peter 3:18 (KJV)

35 - **1** He that dwelleth in the secret place of the Most High Shall abide under the shadow of the Almighty. **2** I will say of Jehovah, He is my refuge and my fortress; My God, in whom I trust. **3** For he will deliver thee from the snare of the fowler, And from the deadly pestilence. **4** He will cover thee with his pinions, and under his wings shalt thou take refuge: His truth is a shield and a buckler. **5** Thou shalt not be afraid for the terror by night, Nor for the arrow that flieth by day; **6** For the pestilence that walketh in darkness, Nor for the destruction that wasteth at noonday. **7** A thousand shall fall at thy side, and ten thousand at thy right hand; *But* it shall not come nigh thee. **8** Only with thine eyes shalt thou behold and see the reward of the wicked.

Their habitation

9 For thou, O Jehovah, art my refuge! Thou hast made the Most High thy habitation; **10** There shall no evil befall thee, Neither shall any plague come nigh thy tent. **11** For he will give his angels charge over thee, To keep thee in all thy ways. **12** They shall bear thee up in their hands, Lest thou dash thy foot against a stone. **13** Thou shalt tread upon the lion and adder: The young lion and the serpent shalt thou trample under foot. **14** Because he hath set his love upon me, therefore will I deliver him: I will set him on high, because he hath known my name. **15** He shall call upon me, and I will answer him; I will be with him in trouble: I will deliver him and honor him. **16** With long life will I satisfy him and show him my salvation.

Psalms 91:1-16 (ASV)

36 - ²⁵ And let us not neglect our meeting together, as some people do, but encourage one another, especially now that the day of his return is drawing near.

Heb 10:25 (NLT)

37 - ²⁶ Mark out a straight path for your feet; stay on the safe path.

Prov 4:26 (NLT)

38 - ³³ Seek the Kingdom of God above all else, and live righteously, and he will give you everything you need.

Matt 6:33 (NLT)

IV. Plant the Seed – Garden for growth

39 - ¹⁵ And the LORD God took the man and put him into the garden of Eden to dress it and to keep it. ¹⁶ And the LORD God commanded the man, saying, of every tree of the garden thou mayest freely eat:

Gen 2:15-16 (KJV)

40 - ¹ I beseech you therefore, brethren, by the mercies of God, to present your bodies a living sacrifice, holy, acceptable to God, *which is* your spiritual service. ² And be not fashioned according to this world: but be ye transformed

by the renewing of your mind, and ye may prove what is the good and acceptable and perfect will of God.

Romans 12:1-2 (ASV)

41 - [24] Another parable set he before them, saying, The kingdom of heaven is likened unto a man that sowed good seed in his field: [25] but while men slept, his enemy came and sowed tares also among the wheat, and went away. [26] But when the blade sprang up and brought forth fruit, then appeared the tares also. [27] And the servants of the householder came and said unto him, Sir, didst thou not sow good seed in thy field? whence then hath it tares? [28] And he said unto them, an enemy hath done this. And the servants say unto him, Wilt thou then that we go and gather them up? [29] But he saith, Nay; lest haply while ye gather up the tares, ye root up the wheat with them. [30] Let both grow together until the harvest: and in the time of the harvest I will say to the reapers, Gather up first the tares, and bind them in bundles to burn them; but gather the wheat into my barn. [31] Another parable set he before them, saying, The kingdom of heaven is like unto a grain of mustard seed, which a man took, and sowed in his field: [32] which indeed is less than all seeds; but when it is grown, it is greater than the herbs, and becometh a tree, so that the birds of the heaven come and lodge in the branches thereof. [33] Another parable spake he unto them; The kingdom of heaven is like unto leaven, which a woman took, and hid in three measures of meal, till it was all leavened.

Matt 13:24-33 (ASV)

42 - [10] God's purpose in all this was to use the church to display his wisdom in its rich variety to all the unseen rulers and authorities in the heavenly places.

Eph 3:10 (NLT)

43 - [17] Then Christ will make his home in your hearts as you trust in him. Your roots will grow down into God's love and keep you strong.

Eph 3:17 (NLT)

44 - [30] Jesus said, "How can I describe the Kingdom of God? What story should I use to illustrate it?[31] It is like a mustard seed planted in the ground. It is the smallest of all seeds,[32] but it becomes the largest of all garden plants; it grows long branches, and birds can make nests in its shade."

Mark 4:30-32 (NLT)

45 - [25] I have been young, and *now* am old; yet have I not seen the righteous forsaken, nor his seed begging bread.

Psalms 37:25 (KJV)

46 - [19] What? know ye not that your body is the temple of the Holy Ghost *which is* in you, which ye have of God, and ye are not your own?

1 Cor 6:19 (KJV)

V. Our God is so transparent; on the six day he stated: "let us make man in our own image":

47 - **26** And God said, Let us make man in our image, after our likeness: and let them have dominion over the fish of the sea, and over the birds of the heavens, and over the cattle, and over all the earth, and over every creeping thing that creepeth upon the earth.

Gen 1:26 (ASV)

48 - **15** No longer do I call you servants; for the servant knoweth not what his lord doeth: but I have called you friends; for all things that I heard from my Father, I have made known unto you.

John 15:15 (ASV)

49 - **35** Jesus replied, "My light will shine for you just a little longer. Walk in the light while you can, so the darkness will not overtake you. Those who walk in the darkness cannot see where they are going. **36** Put your trust in the light while there is still time; then you will become children of the light."

John 12:35-36 (NLT)

50 - **15** Let all who are spiritually mature agree on these things. If you disagree on some point, I believe God will make it plain to you. **16** But we must hold on to the progress we have already made.

Phil 3:15-16 (NLT)

51 - ¹² For we are not fighting against flesh-and-blood enemies, but against evil rulers and authorities of the unseen world, against mighty powers in this dark world, and against evil spirits in the heavenly places. ¹³ Therefore, put on every piece of God's armor so you will be able to resist the enemy in the time of evil. Then after the battle you will still be standing firm.

Eph 6:12-13 (NLT)

52 - ¹² Therefore, as through one-man sin entered into the world, and death through sin; and so death passed unto all men, for that all sinned: —

Romans 5:12 (ASV)

53 - ²² But don't just listen to God's word. You must do what it says. Otherwise, you are only fooling yourselves

James 1:22 (NLT)

54 - ²⁴ No man can serve two masters: for either he will hate the one and love the other; or else he will hold to the one, and despise the other. Ye cannot serve God and mammon.

Matt 6:24 (KJV)

55 - ³ Your gold and silver have become worthless. The very wealth you were counting on will eat away your flesh like fire. This treasure you have accumulated will stand as evidence against you on the day of judgment.

James 5:3 (NLT)

56 - **19** Don't you realize that your body is the temple of the Holy Spirit, who lives in you and was given to you by God? You do not belong to yourself,**20** for God bought you with a high price. So, you must honor God with your body.

1 Cor 6:19-20 (NLT)

57 - **16** *This* I say then, Walk in the Spirit, and ye shall not fulfil the lust of the flesh.

Gal 5:16 (KJV)

58 - **22** But the Holy Spirit produces this kind of fruit in our lives: love, joy, peace, patience, kindness, goodness, faithfulness,**23** gentleness, and self-control. There is no law against these things!

Gal 5:22-23 (NLT)

59 - **7** Let us be glad and rejoice and give honor to him: for the marriage of the Lamb is come, and his wife hath made herself ready.

Rev 19:7 (KJV)

60 - **38** Peter replied, "Each of you must repent of your sins, turn to God, and be baptized in the name of Jesus Christ to show that you have received forgiveness for your sins. Then you will receive the gift of the Holy Spirit.

Acts 2:38 (NLT)

61 - So belief *cometh* of hearing, and hearing by the word of Christ.

Romans 10:17 (ASV)

62 - ⁸ O taste and see that the LORD *is* good: blessed *is* the man *that* trusteth in him.

Psalms 34:8 (KJV)

63 - ¹⁰ Fear of the LORD is the foundation of wisdom. Knowledge of the Holy One results in good judgment.

Prov 9:10 (NLT)

64 - ³ But the Lord is faithful, who shall establish you, and guard you from the evil *one*.

2 Thess 3:2-3 (ASV)

65 - ³ All praise to God, the Father of our Lord Jesus Christ, who has blessed us with every spiritual blessing in the heavenly realms because we are united with Christ

Eph 1:3 (NLT)

66 - ¹ In the beginning was the Word, and the Word was with God, and the Word was God.

John 1:1 (KJV)

67 - **18** Now all of us can come to the Father through the same Holy Spirit because of what Christ has done for us.

Eph 2:18 (NLT)

68 - **1** In the beginning the Word already existed. The Word was with God,

John 1:1 (NLT)

69 - **14** And the Word became flesh and dwelt among us (and we beheld his glory, glory as of the only begotten from the Father), full of grace and truth.

John 1:14 (ASV)

70 - **3** So I want you to know that no one speaking by the Spirit of God will curse Jesus, and no one can say Jesus is Lord, except by the Holy Spirit.

1 Cor 12:3 (NLT)

Printed in the United States
By Bookmasters